BECAUSE HE LOVED ME

BECAUSE HE LOVED ME

By CELINDA GOBELOFF

Because He Loved Me

Paperback ISBN: 979-8-234-00872-5
ASIN:

Publishing and Design:

Ordering Information: Quantity sales. Special discounts are available on quantity purchases by corporations, associations, and others. Orders by U.S. trade bookstores and wholesalers. For details, contact the publisher below:

Please contact: 605-880-1649 | hello@heathers-coaching.com | Heathers-Coaching.com/page/about-cfi-publishing

-This book is dedicated to my husband,
Bobby—
a man whose laughter could fill a room,
whose heart was bigger than life,
and whose love shaped every part of who I am today.
He was more than my husband—
he was my partner, my protector,
my biggest supporter,
and the love of my life.
Everything I am today
is because he loved me.

Table of Contents

Prologue

I didn't know that the last birthday Bobby would give me would also be the day I said goodbye to him.

That morning, the nurses moved quietly around our bedroom, their voices low, their hands gentle. The room smelled like clean sheets and medication, and the music playing softly in the background was his own voice—songs he loved to hear himself sing. I sat beside him, holding his hand, watching his chest rise and fall, rise and fall, each breath feeling more fragile than the last.

For three months, hospice had told us he wouldn't last a week.

For three months, Bobby proved them wrong.

He laughed. He ate. He sang. He came home.

And then, on July 12—my birthday—the man who had never once let that day pass without celebration let go of my hand and slipped quietly into eternity.

If you had asked me years earlier how my story would end, I would have told you it was about love. About music. About faith and laughter and a man whose voice could fill a room and make everyone inside it feel seen. I wouldn't have told you it was about hospital rooms and MRIs. About a doctor saying the words "Stage 4 bladder cancer" like they were just another line in a chart. I wouldn't have told you it was about learning how to give medication schedules, or how to recognize the sound of someone transitioning, or how to sleep beside the person you love knowing they may never wake up again.

And yet—this story is all of that.

It's about the moment life quietly shifts and never returns to what it was. It's about the faith you cling to when answers don't come. It's about loving someone deeply enough to walk them home—and learning how to keep living after they're gone.

Before Bobby became a memory I carry, he was a presence. A force. A voice that could make strangers feel like family and make pain feel lighter, even when his own body was failing him. Before grief had a name in my body, there was music. There was laughter. There was a love I believed would last a lifetime.

This book is the story of how that love carried us through diagnosis, decline, and goodbye—and how God met me in the aftermath, even when the ending wasn't the one I prayed for.

Chapter 1

When Love Found Me

"I have found the one whom my soul loves."—
Song of Solomon 3:4

IF SOMEONE HAD told me years ago that I'd one day be writing a book about finding strength after profound loss and heartbreak, I probably would've laughed and said, "That's not my story." Because back then, my story was about laughter, music, and falling in love with the man who made me feel like the whole world could fit inside one song.

Bobby wasn't just any man—he was magnetic. The kind of person who could walk into a room and instantly lift the energy. He had that smile, that laugh, that voice. I still remember the first time I heard him sing. There was something about the way he looked at me when he was on stage—like even though there were a hundred people in the crowd, I was the only one he saw. That look would stay with me for the rest of my life.

We met through friends, but it felt more like God had written it into the script long before we knew it. He was charming, confident, and funny in that natural way that made people feel comfortable. I was drawn in immediately. What started as casual conversations quickly became long talks about dreams, family, and faith. It was the kind of connection that didn't need forcing—it just flowed.

Before long, we were inseparable. We had that kind of love that wasn't perfect, but it was real. We learned each other's quirks and flaws, laughed through the chaos of life, and found a rhythm that worked for us. Bobby had a way of reminding me not to take life too seriously. Even when things got tough, he'd crack a joke or sing a song to make me smile. He was my calm and my storm, all in one.

And while Bobby didn't have a lot of faith in the way that I did, he always respected mine. He never stood in the way of me bringing God into our home. If anything, he made room for it—whether it was saying grace before dinner, letting me take our daughter to church, or just listening quietly when I talked about what I believed. That kind of quiet acceptance was his way of showing love. It wasn't about religion for him; it was about the heart. And he had one of the biggest hearts I've ever known.

Looking back, I can see how God's hand was in every moment of our love story. There was something sacred about the timing of it all—like He knew we'd need each other for what was coming later, even when we didn't.

Bobby and I built a life filled with laughter, music, and memories. We weren't perfect, but we were perfectly us. I didn't know it then, but those early days—the laughter, the songs, the inside jokes—were the roots that would one day hold me steady when everything else fell apart.

Sometimes God sends people into our lives not just to love us, but to teach us what love really means. Looking back, I see that every moment with Bobby was a gift—one that would later remind me that love doesn't end when life does. It carries on, changing form but never fading. Even when our faiths looked different, God used our love to write a story that only He could have planned.

From My Heart to Yours…

There is something I want to say to you, friend—woman to woman, heart to heart—because if you are holding this book in your hands, chances are you have loved deeply too.

And if you have loved deeply, you have also felt the ache that comes when life shifts in ways you never planned.

I want you to know this first: the love you have experienced—whether it lasted a season or a lifetime—was never wasted. Not one laugh. Not one tear. Not one quiet moment where you felt seen and known. God does not waste love. He uses it. He multiplies it. He plants it deep within you so that one day, when everything feels uncertain, those roots hold.

Song of Solomon says, "I have found the one whom my soul loves." And if you've ever had that kind of love, you understand—it's not just about romance. It's about connections. It's about being known in a way that reaches beyond words. It's about the kind of love that changes you.

But here is the part we don't always talk about...

What happens when that chapter closes?

What happens when the person who was part of your everyday life is no longer there in the same way?

What happens when the laughter quiets, the house feels different, or the life you built no longer looks the way you thought it would?

For many women—especially in this season of life—reinvention doesn't come as a choice. It comes as a moment. A shift. A loss. A realization that something has changed, and you can't go back to who you used to be.

And that can feel overwhelming.

But I want to gently remind you of something that may change the way you see your story...

Reinvention is not loss—it's calling.

The love you experienced was not the end of your story. It was preparation for what is still to come.

Ecclesiastes 3:11 says, "He has made everything beautiful in its time." Not everything is beautiful in the moment. Not everything makes sense while you're walking through it. But God is still working—still writing—still redeeming.

The laughter you shared...
The strength you built together...
The memories that live inside of you...

Those are not things you leave behind. Those are things you carry forward.

You are not starting over from nothing.
You are starting again from experience, from depth, from a love that has shaped you in ways no one can take away.

And maybe right now, you don't feel strong.

Maybe you feel like you're standing in the middle of a life you didn't expect, wondering what comes next.

If that's you, I want to tell you this with all the warmth and encouragement I can:

You are not behind.
You are not forgotten.
And you are certainly not finished.

God is not looking at your life and saying, "That was it."
He is saying, "There is more."

Isaiah 43:19 reminds us, "See, I am doing a new thing! Now it springs up; do you not perceive it?"

Sometimes the "new thing" doesn't look exciting at first. Sometimes it looks like quiet mornings, unanswered questions, or learning how to stand on your own in ways you never had to before.

But even there—especially there—God is moving.

The same God who brought love into your life is the God who is guiding you now.

And here is what I believe with all my heart...

The love you experienced did not end.
It expanded.

It lives in the way you see people now.
It lives in the compassion you carry.
It lives in the strength you didn't know you had until you needed it.

And it will live in what you do next.

Because there is still purpose in you.
There is still joy ahead of you.

There are still chapters waiting to be written—chapters that may look different than you imagined, but are no less meaningful.

So if you are standing in a place of transition—whether it came through loss, change, or a quiet nudge in your spirit—I want you to hear this like a gentle hand on your shoulder:

You are allowed to remember.
You are allowed to grieve.
And you are also allowed to begin again.

You don't have to rush.
You don't have to have all the answers.
You just have to take the next step.

God will meet you there.

And one day, you may look back—just like this—and realize that what felt like an ending...
was actually the beginning of something sacred, something purposeful, something only He could have written.

You have loved.
And because of that, you are more than capable of living fully again.

This next chapter is not replacing what was.

It is building on it.

And there is still so much life—beautiful, meaningful, God-breathed life—waiting for you.

Chapter 2

The Pre-Cana Promise

"And now these three remain: faith, hope and love. But the greatest of these is love."
— 1 Corinthians 13:13

BEFORE WE SAID I do, Bobby and I went through Pre-Cana—the marriage-preparation classes our church required. I'll be honest: he went kicking and screaming. The idea of sitting in a church basement listening to people talk about marriage wasn't exactly his thing. But because he loved me, he agreed—though not without a few dramatic sighs and playful grumbles.

The funny thing is, before long he was the one everybody liked and talked to. That was Bobby. He had a gift for making people laugh and feel comfortable. By the second session, he had the priest laughing, the couples chatting, and somehow managed to turn a serious class into a comedy show. I'd roll my eyes and laugh under my breath because I knew exactly what he was doing—turning charm into connection.

One day during the sessions, they gave us an assignment: Write a love letter to each other.
I remember thinking, Oh no, I'm not good at this kind of thing.
I wrote the basics: I love you, and I'm so glad we're building a life together. Sweet, simple, from the heart—but nothing fancy.

Then Bobby handed me his. It was a full-page letter. I was shocked. It was so beautiful and heartfelt, I could hardly believe it came from the same man who cracked jokes all through class. The words were tender, poetic, and full of emotion. I remember reading it and feeling my eyes well up, thinking, Wow ... he really does feel this deeply.

About a year later, my parents came to visit. We were sitting at dinner, laughing and catching up, when out of nowhere Bobby looked at me and said,"Hey, do you still have that notebook from Pre-Cana? The one with our letters?"

I nodded, a little confused. "Yeah, why?"

He said, "Go get it."

So I did. I brought it out, thinking he wanted to reread the letter or show my parents how sweet he was. He opened the notebook, grinned, and said, "Listen to this ..."
And then he started singing.

It turns out that beautiful love letter he wrote? It was the lyrics to 'You Make Me Feel Brand New' by The Stylistics.

I couldn't believe it. I said, "Bobby! You didn't write that—you copied a song!"

He just laughed that big laugh of his and said, "Well, it said everything I wanted to say, didn't it?"

My parents and I burst out laughing. It became one of those family stories that lived on for years—one of those moments that perfectly summed him up. That was Bobby—equal parts heart and humor. He might have gone to Pre-Cana kicking and screaming, but by the end he was the star of the class and had everyone falling in love with his spirit, just like I did.

At the very end of the course, the priest gave us a message that has stayed with me my entire life. He said,
"Some of you will last, and some of you will not. God brings us together through attraction—to love one another. But what you do with that love after the attraction fades will determine how your marriage will go. If you still feel like you need to keep going out to find that feeling again, your marriage will never last. But if you learn how to love that person for who they are and respect each other through faith and family, your marriage will endure."

Those words never left me. Even then, before all the challenges and heartache that would come, I knew he was right. Real love isn't just butterflies and excitement—it's the quiet decision, every day, to stay, to forgive, to build, and to believe in something bigger than yourself.

In the years that followed, I watched those words come to life. Our marriage wasn't perfect, but it was strong because we practiced what we learned there—communication, respect, laughter, and grace. God used that little church basement to plant seeds that would carry us through seasons of joy and through the storms that lay ahead. What Bobby took from this was mutual respect, if there was a problem or an issue, we would stop what we were doing and talk about it. And date night through a whole marriage was very important to him and we tried to do it once a week every week with just him and I connected us a couple and what was important to our marriage.

Love isn't about chasing the feeling—it's about choosing the person. The priest's words from Pre-Cana still echo in my heart: attraction might bring two people together, but it's faith, respect, and everyday grace that keep them there. God doesn't just write love stories; He teaches us how to live them.

From My Heart to Yours…

I want to pause here and speak to you—not just as someone reading a story, but as a woman who has lived enough life to know that love is never as simple as we once imagined it would be.

If you've made it this far, you've likely had your own version of a "Pre-Cana moment." Maybe it wasn't in a church basement. Maybe it wasn't a class at all. But somewhere along the way, you stepped into a relationship, a commitment, or a season of life believing that love would carry you through.

And it does… just not always in the way we expect.

In the beginning, love often feels effortless. It's laughter across a dinner table, inside jokes, songs that mean something only to the two of you. It's the butterflies, the excitement, the feeling that you've found something special—something chosen just for you.

And in many ways, you have.

But what we don't always realize in those early moments is that love isn't just a feeling we fall into. It's a life we grow into.

That priest's words—"what you do with that love after the attraction fades..."—they hold more truth than we often understand at the time.

Because life has a way of stretching love.

There are seasons when it's easy to choose each other...
And there are seasons when choosing takes everything you have.

There are moments filled with laughter...
And others filled with silence, distance, or even loss.

And for many women in this season of life, the question quietly shifts from "How do I love this person?" to something deeper:

"What does love look like now?"

Maybe your story includes years of marriage.
Maybe it includes heartbreak, divorce, or loss.
Maybe it includes waking up one day and realizing the life you built has changed—and you're not quite sure who you are without it.

If that's where you find yourself, I want to gently remind you of something that may steady your heart:

Love did not fail you.

It formed you.

Every time you chose to stay...
Every time you forgave...
Every time you showed up when it would have been easier to walk away...

You were becoming someone stronger, deeper, and more capable than you even realized.

1 Corinthians 13:13 tells us, "And now these thr*ee remain: faith, hope and love. But the greatest of these is love."*

Not the kind of love that is based on feelings alone...
But the kind that is built, refined, and strengthened over time.

The kind that teaches you patience.
The kind that teaches you grace.
The kind that, even when life changes, never truly leaves you.

Because here's the truth that I believe God wants you to hear in this moment:

The love you learned is still yours to carry.

Even if the relationship has changed...
Even if the person is no longer beside you...
Even if the life you once knew looks completely different...

The capacity you built to love—to care, to show up, to believe in something bigger than yourself—that did not disappear.

It lives inside of you.

And it will be part of what shapes what comes next.

This is where reinvention begins to take on a new meaning.

It's not about replacing what you had.
It's not about going back and trying to recreate a feeling.

It's about stepping forward with everything love has already taught you.

It's about understanding that the same woman who built a life, who loved deeply, who walked through both joy and challenge... is still here.

And she is not done.

Romans 5:3–4 says, *"We also glory in our sufferings, because we know that suffering produces perseverance; perseverance, character; and character, hope."*

Hope.

Not the kind of hope that looks backward wishing things were different...
But the kind that looks forward and says, *"There is still something ahead of me."*

So if you are in a season where things feel uncertain—where love looks different than it once did, or where you're learning how to stand in a new version of your life—I want you to hear this like a quiet truth settling into your spirit:

You are not starting over from nothing.
You are moving forward with everything love has already built in you.

The laughter, the lessons, the grace, the resilience...
They are not behind you.

They are within you.

And God, in His perfect way, is not asking you to go find something you've lost...

He is inviting you to step into what you've been prepared for.

Because reinvention—this season you're in right now—is not the absence of love.

It is the continuation of it.

Just in a new form.

Chapter 3

Building a Life Together

"By wisdom a house is built, and through understanding it is established; through knowledge its rooms are filled with rare and beautiful treasures."

— Proverbs 24:3–4

AFTER PRE-CANA, Bobby and I stepped into marriage with excitement, hope, and a touch of "let's see what happens." We didn't have everything figured out, but we had love — and a lot of laughter. That combination carried us through more than either of us could have imagined.

When we first got married, we lived in New Jersey. Bobby was still playing in his band, so our weekends were spent at his gigs.

I worked full-time during the week and sometimes weekends in retail, so our schedules were busy — but somehow, we made it work. Our life was full. There was always music, friends, and family around us. Bobby loved being on stage, and I loved watching him do what he loved. Those were loud, joyful days — the kind that felt like they'd last forever.

A few years later, we decided to make a big move. My family had relocated to Virginia Beach, and we wanted to be close to them. So we packed up and headed south. We stayed with my parents for about a year while we got settled, and with my father's help, we eventually bought our first home. At that point, we had been married about five years — still dreaming, still laughing, and still hoping for a baby.

We had been trying to get pregnant all those years, and after a while, I began to wonder if maybe it just wasn't meant to be. Then, when I least expected it, I found out I was pregnant. God's timing, not mine. We were blessed with a beautiful baby girl — our miracle. From the moment she arrived, she became the absolute light of our lives. Everything changed in the best possible way.

We moved into a nice community, the kind where everyone knew everyone. Some of our neighbors joked that we must be in the Witness Protection Program because of our New York accents. Others thought maybe we were in the mob! We used to laugh so hard about that. Bobby would lean into it just for fun, throwing in his "New Yawk" charm and making people laugh even more. That was his gift — he never met a stranger.

Bobby eventually started his own business. At first, he built houses and additions, and then he got into painting. He made plenty of friends through his work — good friends, the kind that last a lifetime. He was always the one people called when they needed help. I used to call him "The Fixer." If something was broken — a sink, a fence, or even someone's spirit — Bobby was there. He couldn't help himself; helping others was just part of who he was.

Even though his parents lived in California, he loved my family like his own. My sisters were his sisters, my brother and cousins were his too. If we went out together, he always looked out for everyone. He'd call my parents "Mom" and "Dad," and every Thanksgiving, he'd write a poem about everything that had happened during the year. Sometimes it was sweet, sometimes it was funny — and sometimes it was a little embarrassing! But that was Bobby. Whatever popped into his head came straight out of his mouth — no filter, ever. And that's exactly why everyone loved him.

And while Bobby could act like a tough guy — especially around friends and family — I always got to see the soft side that few others did. People would sometimes say, "Oh my goodness, how do you put up with him?" and I'd just smile. Because at home, he was a teddy bear. He brought me coffee in bed every morning. He made breakfast for us on the weekends. If I worked late, dinner was ready when I got home.

The day I found out I was pregnant, he refused to let me lift a finger. From that day on, he took over the vacuuming — and never gave it back! If I ever said I wanted to do something around the house, like power wash the deck or blow the leaves, he'd just shrug and say, "Okay, go ahead." I could count to five before he'd be outside taking care of it himself. That was Bobby — a mix of stubbornness and love. Even when I wanted to do things my way, he couldn't help but step in and make sure I didn't have to.

Family and tradition were everything to him. Holidays were sacred, filled with laughter, food, and gratitude. Every New Year's Eve, we hosted a big party — friends, family, neighbors — our home bursting with joy and music. Those nights were some of my favorite memories, watching Bobby make everyone feel welcome and loved.

I'll never forget our first argument — I can't even remember what it was about — but the next morning, when I came into the kitchen, there was a note on the table. It said, *"Never forget the things that brought us together in the first place."*
To this day, that note is still hanging on my refrigerator.

Bobby always had a special bond with my father. About ten years ago, he invited my dad to dinner one Friday night, and it turned into a tradition. Every Friday, the two of them — along with a few of my dad's friends and sometimes family members — would go out to dinner and smoke cigars afterward. It became *their thing*. Those nights meant the world to both of them.

Through the years, we built our careers and raised our daughter together. When she was seven, she was diagnosed with Type 2 diabetes. It was devastating at first, but we learned to manage it together, and she has continued to thrive despite it. We were so proud of her strength — and it only brought us closer as a family.

Then one day, Bobby came home with a motorcycle. Just like that. No warning, no big talk — just that Bobby grin and a set of keys. I was nervous, of course, but I rode with him a few times. And, as always, he made it fun. Through riding, he met a whole new group of wonderful people who became lifelong friends. The motorcycle community became an extended family to us — full of love, laughter, and support. Even today, many of those friendships remain.

Our marriage wasn't perfect, but it was *real*. We had our share of disagreements — money, work, whose turn it was to do what — but the lessons from Pre-Cana always seemed to find their way back into our hearts. When tempers flared, one of us would break the tension with a smile or a joke. Most of the time, it was Bobby. He could make me laugh even when I didn't want to, and I could never stay mad for long.

Even though Bobby didn't have the same level of faith that I did, he always respected mine. On Sundays when I wanted to go to church, he'd grin and say, "You go talk to your guy upstairs. I'll have coffee waiting when you get back." That was his quiet way of loving me. He might not have prayed out loud, but he showed love in action — the way he cared, protected, and supported me.

Looking back, I can see how God was building a foundation in those ordinary years. Through laughter, patience, and forgiveness, He was shaping our love into something resilient. We didn't know it then, but every shared meal, every quiet night, every storm we weathered together was preparing us for the bigger challenges we would one day face.

The strongest marriages aren't built in the big moments — they're built in the everyday acts of love. The coffee in bed, the shared laughter, the small traditions, and the quiet forgiveness — those were the bricks of our foundation. God uses ordinary days to prepare us for extraordinary strength. Looking back, I can see His fingerprints in every detail of our life — from the music and laughter to the challenges that refined our love into something lasting and true.

From My Heart to Yours...

I want to sit with you here for a moment, because this chapter—the building, the everyday, the ordinary—this is where so much of your life has likely been lived too.

Not in the big milestones...
But in the quiet, repeated moments that didn't seem extraordinary at the time.

The mornings you got up and did what needed to be done.
The meals you made.
The conversations you had around kitchen tables.
The routines, the responsibilities, the rhythms of a life built over years.

That's where love really lives.

Proverbs reminds us, "By wisdom a house is built... through knowledge its rooms are filled with rare and beautiful treasures."

And when I read that now, I don't just think about a physical house. I think about a life.

A life like the one you may have built.

One filled with memories that don't always look like much from the outside... but inside? They are everything.

The laughter that echoed through your home.
The traditions you created.
The people who walked in and out of your doors and felt something warm, something safe, something real.

Those are the treasures.

And here's what I know to be true...

You don't always realize you're building something extraordinary while you're living it.

At the time, it just feels like life.

But one day, you look back—and you see it differently.

You see the way God was present in the details.
You see how the small things were actually the big things.
You see how the ordinary days were quietly shaping a foundation strong enough to carry you through more than you ever expected.

And maybe, like me... you didn't know just how strong that foundation would need to be.

Because life has a way of changing.

Children grow up.
Careers shift.
Relationships evolve.
Loss enters where you never thought it would.

And suddenly, the life you spent years building doesn't look the same anymore.

If you're in that place right now—where things feel different, quieter, or even uncertain—I want you to hear this in a way that settles deep in your heart:

Nothing you built was lost.

It was established.

Every act of love...
Every sacrifice...
Every moment you chose your family, your marriage, your people...

It created something inside of you that cannot be taken away.

Strength.
Resilience.
Depth.
And a capacity to love that only comes from living it out day after day.

You may not be living in the same season anymore...
But you are still the woman who built that life.

And that matters more than you realize.

Because reinvention—this next chapter you may be stepping into—is not about leaving that life behind.

It's about carrying forward everything it gave you.

The patience you learned.
The grace you practiced.
The way you show up for others without even thinking twice.

Those are not things you start over on.

Those are things you build from.

Psalm 127:1 says, "Unless the Lord builds the house, the builders labor in vain."

But friend... your house was not built in vain.

God was there in the laughter.
He was there in the long days and the late nights.
He was there in the challenges that stretched you and the moments that filled your heart to the brim.

And He is still there now.

Even if the house feels quieter...
Even if the roles you once held have shifted...
Even if you're wondering what your life is supposed to look like next...

God is not finished building.

He is just building something new... with the same strong, faithful woman He has been shaping all along.

So if you find yourself looking back, missing what was, or wondering if your most meaningful days are behind you…

Let me gently remind you:

They are not behind you.

They are within you.

Everything you built—every memory, every lesson, every act of love—has prepared you for this season.

And this season?

It still holds purpose.
It still holds joy.
It still holds opportunities to create, to connect, to love again in new and meaningful ways.

You are not stepping into something empty.

You are stepping into something that is built on a lifetime of love.

And that is one of the most powerful places a woman can begin again.

Because reinvention is not about starting from scratch…

It's about rising from a foundation that was already filled with rare and beautiful treasures.

And you, my friend, are one of them.

Chapter 4

When Life Changed

"When you pass through the waters, I will be with you; and through the rivers, they shall not overwhelm you. When you walk through the fire, you shall not be burned, and the flame shall not consume you."

— Isaiah 43:2

LIFE HAS A WAY OF SHIFTING when you least expect it. One moment everything feels normal — full of routines, plans, laughter — and the next, you're holding your breath, praying that what's happening isn't as serious as it seems.

For years, Bobby had been living with COPD. He managed it as best he could, always keeping up with his doctor visits and doing what he was told. But over time, his breathing issues grew worse. There were days he'd get winded just walking across the room, and I could see the frustration in his eyes — not because he was scared, but because he hated feeling weak. He'd joke about it, brush it off, but I knew better.

Then he started losing weight, and that's when I began to worry more. He looked thinner, tired, but still pushed through each day. His doctor brushed it off as "just getting older." His blood work looked fine, and I'll never forget the doctor saying, "If it wasn't for your COPD, you'd be a twenty-year-old." At the time, I wanted to believe that. I wanted to hold on to any words that sounded normal.

But things didn't get better. He began having breathing attacks so severe that I had to take him to the emergency room — twice. Both times they said it was partly due to his COPD, and partly anxiety. Each time, I drove home exhausted but thankful he was still okay, telling myself we'd get it under control.

Then came a new issue — he started needing to go to the bathroom every hour, all night long. It kept him from resting well, and no matter what medication the doctors prescribed for his prostate, nothing helped. He tried to stay strong, but the lack of relief started wearing him down. Then his back pain began.

At first, the doctors said it was degenerative disc disease. They gave him pain medication and told him to rest. But the pain kept getting worse — so bad he couldn't lie down or sit comfortably. I went with him to a follow-up appointment, and I remember the doctor saying they might send him to pain management if it didn't ease up soon. During that visit, they noticed a shadow in his lower abdomen and thought it might be an aneurysm. They said they'd keep an eye on it, but not to worry.

A week later, Bobby called the doctor himself. He said, "This pain isn't just my back. I can't sleep. I can't sit. I can barely walk." So they scheduled an MRI — but it was another ten days before he could get it.

The day of that MRI is burned into my memory. I drove him there, and something in me felt off — like I knew this was the start of something bigger. On the way home, I looked over at him and said softly, "I feel like this is the beginning of the end." He reached over, put his hand on mine, and said, "Don't worry, honey. I'm not going anywhere yet."

Later that night, his pain became unbearable. I called 911. At the hospital, they thought maybe he was passing kidney stones. For a moment, we were almost relieved — thinking, thank God, it's something simple. But about an hour and a half later, the doctor came back into the room, and the look on his face told me before he even spoke.

He said the words that stopped my world:
"It's bladder cancer." Stage 4.

I can still hear that moment in my head — the hum of the machines, the sound of the curtain swaying as the doctor walked out, the silence between us. We were in shock. We were exhausted. But somehow, Bobby reached for my hand and said, "We'll fight this. We'll beat this."

That was him — strong, stubborn, and full of hope even when he was scared.

We went home that night clinging to faith and each other. We talked about what might come next, and in that quiet moment, I asked him if I could have his last rites blessed over him — not because I was giving up, but because I wanted him to be protected, covered by faith no matter what happened. He agreed. That was Bobby's heart — loving me enough to honor what mattered to me most.

The next day, the hospital called and told us he needed another MRI. We went back, and after waiting nearly five hours, Bobby was in so much pain he said, "Forget this. I can't sit here anymore." We left. The next morning, the doctor called again — they wanted to start radiation and then move on to chemo. We thought, okay, there's a plan. We can do this.

But then, everything changed again. The doctor called back and said Bobby needed to come into the hospital by ambulance — immediately. The tumor had wrapped around his spine, and they were afraid he could become paralyzed.

He was admitted to one hospital, but we had to wait three days for a transfer to another facility that could perform the surgery. During that time, he stayed strong — joking with the nurses, reassuring me, telling me not to worry. He was on medication that helped manage his pain, but I could see the toll it was taking.

When he finally had the surgery, we thought it would give him relief — maybe even buy us more time. But that surgery changed everything. He made it through, but he was never truly able to walk again.

I'll never forget sitting by his hospital bed, looking at his hands — the same hands that had built homes, made breakfast, and held mine through so much life. I remember thinking, How is this happening? But even then, he still found ways to make me laugh. He'd tell the nurses jokes, tease me when I'd start to cry, and somehow, even in that hospital room, he filled the space with love.

That was Bobby — brave, unfiltered, full of life until the very end. And in those moments, I realized that faith doesn't always look like loud prayers or perfect peace. Sometimes, faith is just sitting beside the person you love, holding their hand, and whispering, We'll get through this somehow.

Life can turn upside down in a single moment, but faith steadies the soul when everything else shakes. Even when fear tried to take over, love and faith stood taller. We didn't know how long we had, but we knew Who was walking with us through the fire.

And if something doesn't feel right — make your doctors dig deeper. Bobby put a lot of faith in his doctors, and we trusted that everything they said was the whole picture. But his constant pain wasn't "just his back" or "just his prostate." It was the cancer. Maybe if they had looked closer sooner, things might have been different. Trust your instincts. God gives us that inner voice for a reason — to protect the ones we love.

From My Heart to Yours…

I want to slow this moment down with you, because this is the part of the story that none of us ever plan for.

This is the part where life no longer feels predictable.
Where the ground beneath you shifts, and suddenly everything you thought was steady… isn't.

And if you've lived long enough, you know exactly what I mean.

Because at some point, every woman walks through a moment where life changes in an instant.

A phone call.
A diagnosis.

A loss.
A sentence spoken in a quiet room that echoes louder than anything you've ever heard.

And nothing prepares you for it.

Isaiah 43:2 says, *"When you pass through the waters, I will be with you… when you walk through the fire, you shall not be burned."*

Not *if*.

When.

That's the part we don't always talk about.

We love the idea of faith when life feels good, when everything is working, when the days are full and the nights are peaceful. But real faith—the kind that changes you—shows up in moments like this.

Moments where you don't have answers.
Moments where you don't feel strong.
Moments where all you can do is sit beside someone you love and hold on.

If you are reading this and you've ever walked through something like this—or maybe you're in it right now—I want you to know something that is deeply true:

You are stronger than you feel.

Not because you chose this.
Not because you were ready.

But because God meets you in places you never thought you could survive.

There is a kind of love that only reveals itself in the hard moments.

The love that stays in hospital rooms.
The love that sits through long nights.
The love that whispers prayers when words are hard to find.
The love that chooses presence when there is nothing left to fix.

That kind of love is sacred.

And if you've lived it, you know—it changes you.

It strips away the unimportant things.
It clarifies what really matters.
It shows you the depth of your own heart in ways you didn't even know were possible.

But it also asks something of you.

It asks you to keep going... when you don't know how.
It asks you to trust... when fear is louder than faith.
It asks you to stand... when everything in you feels like it's breaking.

And yet—even there—you are not alone.

Sometimes faith doesn't look like confidence.

Sometimes it looks like tears falling quietly while you hold someone's hand.
Sometimes it looks like asking questions you don't get answers to.

Sometimes it looks like simply staying... when walking away isn't an option.

And that is enough.

Psalm 34:18 tells us, *"The Lord is close to the brokenhearted and saves those who are crushed in spirit."*

Close.

Not distant.
Not waiting for you to be stronger.
Not expecting you to have it all together.

Close in the hospital room.
Close in the silence.
Close in the fear.
Close in the moments where your heart feels like it might not hold everything it's carrying.

And maybe right now, or maybe in your past, you've had a moment where you asked...

How is this happening?
Why didn't we catch it sooner?
Could something have been different?

Those questions are real.
And they come from a place of love.

Because when you love someone deeply, you want to protect them. You want to fix it. You want more time.

But I want to gently remind you of something that may bring a little peace to your heart:

God was there.
Even in the moments that didn't make sense.

Even in the waiting.
Even in the unknown.
Even in the pain.

He did not leave you.

And He did not leave the person you love.

Because here's what I believe with everything in me...

Love and faith stand the tallest in the hardest moments.

Not because everything turns out the way we hoped...
But because even when life changes, love remains.

The laughter may quiet.
The routines may shift.
The future may look different than you imagined.

But the love?

It does not disappear.

It deepens.
It strengthens.
It becomes something eternal.

And you—whether you realize it or not—become someone new in the process.

Not because you wanted to.
But because you walked through the fire and kept going.

That is where reinvention begins, even if you don't recognize it yet.

Not in the moment everything falls apart...
But in the quiet strength that rises within you as you keep showing up, keep loving, keep believing—one breath at a time.

So, if you are in a season where life feels uncertain, where fear has tried to take up space in your heart, where you're holding on and hoping for strength...

Let me say this to you gently, but clearly:

You will get through this.

Not because it's easy.
Not because it's fair.
But because God is with you in it.

And one day—maybe not today, maybe not soon—but one day...

You will look back and see that even in the fire, you were not consumed.

You were carried.

And somehow, through it all...

Love and faith were still standing.

Chapter 5

Holding On to Hope

"The Lord is close to the brokenhearted and saves those who are crushed in spirit."
— Psalm 34:18

THE MONTHS AFTER Bobby's surgery became a blur of hospital rooms, doctors, and prayers. For the first three months, he was in the hospital. He came home briefly in February, and for a few precious days it felt like maybe we'd turned a corner. But then he started having trouble breathing again. He developed pneumonia, and I had to call the ambulance. Back to the hospital he went — another couple of weeks — and then on to rehab.

After the surgery, the oncologist came to visit Bobby. His voice was calm but his words were devastating: "Stage four. There's no cure. We can try to extend your life with radiation and immunotherapy treatments, but we cannot cure this."

I'll never forget the morning Bobby called me, his voice breaking with emotion. He was in tears — the man who always held everything together. He said, "There's no cure." And I said, "We're going to fight. Just because they say it's this long doesn't mean it's this long. I've known people who lived much longer than the doctors predicted."

He started radiation, but because of insurance rules, he was never able to begin full treatment with the oncologist. They required him to physically walk into the oncologist's office for treatment, and they wouldn't treat him in the hospital. The system felt so cruel. A few times they brought up hospice, but I kept saying, "No. My husband needs a fighting chance."

In March, after his surgery, Bobby was sent to a rehab facility to recover and regain some strength. I had hoped it would help him, but it turned out to be one of the worst experiences of all. The staff was terrible — they weren't taking care of people the way they should have been. I felt so bad for most of the patients there. It broke my heart to see how neglected some of them were.

I remember Bobby calling me late one night, his voice tight with pain. He said they weren't giving him his medication, and when he rang for help to use the bathroom, he had to wait over an hour before anyone came. I felt helpless, furious, and heartbroken all at once. He deserved dignity, comfort, and care — not to be treated like he was an inconvenience. That experience at rehab showed me how easily people can fall through the cracks, even when they're fighting for their lives.

Rehab was a nightmare. He wasn't getting better. He was struggling to breathe, and then he caught pneumonia there, too. It felt like we were living in a revolving door of hospitals, waiting rooms, and IV poles. Each time we thought we'd gotten a handle on something, a new complication appeared.

As the weeks dragged on, I began to feel like everyone had quietly given up on him. It was harder for him to walk. Harder for him to breathe. They just kept giving him pain medication. I would sit by his bed, watching the nurse ask, "What's your pain level?" Bobby would give them the highest number, even though he wasn't complaining moments earlier. I'd look at him and think, Why aren't you saying how you really feel? But I think, deep down, he was just done explaining.

I was at the hospital every single day. For three months, that was my life. I felt paralyzed by fear — afraid to ask too many questions, afraid of the answers. Each morning, I'd bring him breakfast. I'd sit with him, watch his vital signs, memorize every rise and fall. Sometimes his numbers looked perfect and I'd feel a flicker of hope, only for it to be crushed by another setback.

At night, when visiting hours were over, I'd stop by my parents' house for dinner and a glass of wine before going home. I never liked being home alone — it was something I'd never had to do. My husband was always there, or my daughter was, and Bobby never liked going anywhere without me. So being alone in that house felt foreign, and honestly, frightening.

I'd get home late, exhausted, but even simple things became hard. I couldn't even take a shower without feeling anxious, so my sister would come over and stay while I did. Some nights I'd talk for hours with my cousins from Long Island, who did their best to make me laugh and lift my spirits — usually over another glass of wine. My sisters took turns sleeping over, and sometimes my daughter would come stay with me too. Those phone calls and sleepovers were my lifeline. They helped me not dwell on what was happening, even if only for a little while.

But even with all that love around me, it was a very isolating experience — the kind of loneliness that sits in your chest no matter who's in the room. I had an incredible village around me, but there's a certain kind of ache only a spouse can fill, and that absence echoed through every quiet moment.

I couldn't understand why they'd bring him to physical therapy right after loading him up with medication. How could they expect him to walk like that? One weekend they gave him so much medication he slept for two days straight. I couldn't wake him. When he finally did wake up, someone just said, "Oops, I think we overmedicated him." My heart sank.

I started asking the doctors, "What are we doing? What's the plan?" They said they'd get together with the medical team. Two days later, they called me back and said there was nothing more they could do.

They could send him home on hospice, but they thought he had about a week to live.

My heart broke.

But through all of it, we were not alone. My sisters came every day, taking turns sitting with me and Bobby. My friend Lori (before she passed) would come to give me breaks. Another friend, also named Lori, would arrive early so I could sleep in. Bobby's good friend Rick was there almost every day. Big John, who worked at the hospital, would check in constantly. My girlfriends came when they could. Friends called to ask if I needed anything. I always said, "I'm good," but in reality, I was drowning.

One day I even went to the doctor myself. I'd been feeling so much anxiety. My blood work came back with a low white blood cell count. It terrified me. I thought, What if I have cancer too? They sent me to a blood oncologist. Thank God, it wasn't cancer — just something that looked more like an allergy, though to this day they've never figured it out. But that moment showed me how thin my own strength had stretched.

The hardest day came when Bobby woke up and we had to tell him he was coming home on hospice. Me, my daughter, and my sisters were there. The doctors said there was nothing more they could do. Bobby looked at us, then simply said, "Get me home." That was Bobby — strong and direct, even at the very end.

Faith held me up when my body and heart felt like they couldn't anymore. God sent people — my sisters, my friends, Bobby's friends — to hold me steady when I was drowning.

And if something doesn't feel right, make your doctors dig deeper. Bobby trusted his doctors, and we did too. But his constant pain wasn't "just his back" or "just his prostate." It was the cancer. Maybe if they had looked closer sooner, things might have been different. Trust your instincts. God gives us that inner voice for a reason — to protect the ones we love.

From My Heart to Yours…

I want to sit beside you in this chapter for a moment, because this is where hope feels the hardest to hold.

Not because you don't believe…
But because everything around you is trying to convince you to let go.

If you've ever walked through a season like this—or if you're in one right now—you know what I mean.

This is the place where days blur together.
Where you measure time in doctor visits, phone calls, and quiet moments of waiting.
Where your heart is constantly pulled between *faith* and *fear*.

You wake up hoping for good news…
And brace yourself for something else.

And somewhere in the middle of all of that, you're trying to stay strong—for them, for your family, for yourself.

But what people don't always see is how heavy that strength really is.

Psalm 34:18 says, *"The Lord is close to the brokenhearted and saves those who are crushed in spirit."*

Crushed.

That word matters.

Because there are seasons in life where "tired" doesn't even begin to describe it.
Where your heart feels stretched so thin you don't know how it's still holding everything.

And yet... it does.

Not because you're superhuman.
Not because you have it all together.

But because God is closer than you realize.

Closer in the hospital rooms.
Closer in the waiting.
Closer in the quiet drives home when your mind won't stop racing.
Closer in the moments when you finally sit down and feel everything hit you all at once.

He is there.

Even when you don't feel Him the way you want to.
Even when your prayers feel more like whispers... or questions... or silence.

And I want to gently say something to you, especially if you've ever felt like you were "barely holding it together" in a season like this:

That *is* faith.

Faith is not always bold declarations and unshakable confidence.

Sometimes faith looks like showing up again the next day.
Sometimes it looks like sitting beside someone you love and simply being there.
Sometimes it looks like saying, *"God, I don't understand this... but I'm still here."*

And that is enough.

But I also want to acknowledge something that doesn't get talked about enough...

Even when you are surrounded by people who love you—family, friends, a whole village showing up for you—there can still be a deep loneliness in this kind of season.

A quiet ache that no one else can quite touch.

Because the person you shared your life with...
The one who filled your days and your home and your heart...

They are the one you want beside you.

And that absence—even when they are still physically there but everything is changing—can feel overwhelming.

If you've felt that, you are not alone in it.

And there is nothing wrong with you for feeling that way.

But here is what I want you to hold onto, even if it's just with the smallest thread of hope:

You are not carrying this by yourself.

God often sends people to hold us up when we don't have the strength to stand.

The sister who shows up.
The friend who calls.
The person who sits with you in silence or makes you laugh when you didn't think you could.

That is not coincidence.

That is God's provision.

Ecclesiastes 4:9–10 says, *"Two are better than one... If either of them falls down, one can help the other up."*

And sometimes, in the hardest seasons, God doesn't just send one.

He sends many.

Not to take the pain away...
But to make sure you don't drown in it.

And maybe right now, or maybe in a season you've already walked through, you've asked questions like:

Why isn't this getting better?
Why does it feel like no one is listening?
Why do I feel like I have to fight for every answer, every step, every ounce of care?

Those questions come from love.

From a heart that refuses to give up.

From a woman who knows—deep down—when something isn't right.

And I want to affirm something that is so important:

That voice inside of you matters.

That instinct.
That nudge.
That feeling that says, *"Something isn't right, I need to ask again."*

God gave you that.

Not to create fear...
But to create awareness.

You are allowed to ask questions.
You are allowed to push for answers.
You are allowed to advocate for the people you love.

That is not doubt.

That is love in action.

And through all of this—through the fear, the exhaustion, the uncertainty—there is one thing that quietly remains:

Hope.

Not the kind of hope that ignores reality...
But the kind that says, *"Even here... God is still present."*

The kind that holds on, even when your hands are tired.
The kind that believes there is still purpose, even when the path looks unclear.

Because hope is not about having control over the outcome.

It's about trusting that you are not alone in the process.

Romans 15:13 says, *"May the God of hope fill you with all joy and peace as you trust in Him..."*

Not as everything goes perfectly.
Not as everything makes sense.

As you trust.

Even a little.
Even when it's hard.
Even when all you can do is whisper His name.

So if you are in a season where you feel like you're barely holding on...

Let me say this to you with all the gentleness and strength I can:

You don't have to hold everything together.

You just have to hold on.

God will hold the rest.

And one day—somehow, some way—you will look back and realize that even in the moments where you felt like you were drowning...

You were being carried.

Because reinvention doesn't begin when everything is fixed.

It begins right here—

In the middle of the storm...
In the middle of the unknown...
In the middle of a woman choosing to keep showing up, keep loving, and keep believing...

Even when it's the hardest thing she's ever done.

Chapter 6

When He Came Home

"The Lord is my shepherd; I shall not want.
He makes me lie down in green pastures,
He leads me beside still waters,
He restores my soul."
— Psalm 23:1–3

WHEN BOBBY CAME HOME on hospice, he was happy.

I'll never forget that.

I had prepared a room for him — a hospital bed, the equipment, everything hospice told me we would need. When he saw it, instead of fear, there was relief. He was home. And home mattered.

Hospice arrived with a long list of medications — what each one was for, when to give it, what to watch for. It was overwhelming. I remember holding the papers and thinking, I don't know if I can do this. I had never taken care of someone this way before. The responsibility felt enormous.

But the nurses came almost every day. They guided me, reassured me, and taught me. Slowly, I began to feel more confident. And something unexpected happened — Bobby started eating better. He enjoyed meals again. Everything I cooked was "the best thing he'd ever had," even when I knew it was simple. Seeing him eat gave me hope. It made me feel like maybe... just maybe... I was doing something right.

Friends and family surrounded us. People showed up constantly — bringing breakfast, lunch, and dinner. Some came to sit and talk with Bobby. Others came just to be present. My girlfriends would stop by with a bottle of wine — sometimes two — and we'd sit together, laughing and reminiscing. My mother & sister came almost every night to sit with me, keeping me company so I wasn't alone.

Sometimes Bobby would come out in his wheelchair and sit with us. We talked. We laughed. For moments at a time, it almost felt normal.

Almost like he was his old self again.

My daughter and my sisters organized a fundraiser for him, and hundreds of people showed up. We got Bobby there in his wheelchair. That night, he sang the song he was known for — Sweet Caroline. The room was filled with love, voices joining in, tears streaming down faces. There wasn't a dry eye in the place. Watching him sing, surrounded by people who loved him, I felt heartbreak and gratitude collide in my chest.

At home, I sat with him watching TV. I made him breakfast, lunch, and dinner — and he ate it all. For nearly two months, I allowed myself to believe things were okay. Maybe not healed — but okay.

The nurses came every other day. Bobby had them laughing nonstop. He handed out his CDs — recordings of all the songs he loved to sing. They adored him. Everyone did.

My daughter and her fiancé moved in to help me, giving me peace of mind I didn't even realize I needed. One weekend, Bobby became very disoriented. The nurses told me he was "transitioning." A substitute nurse came on a Sunday and gently told me it could be a matter of hours.

I was home alone when she left. I felt completely desolate.

That same day, Bobby's regular doctor called just to check on me. I told him what was happening, and he said, "It could be a UTI. Let's try antibiotics." I called hospice, and they got the medication for me. Within twenty-four hours, Bobby was awake again. Talking. Coherent.

Even then, though, I could see the toll it was taking on him.

Friends & Family— mine and his — continued to show up. Fixing things around the house. Bringing meals. Helping get Bobby out of bed so he could sit at the table with us. One day, a few of his close friends brought over a scooter for him. He was pretty medicated at the time and didn't fully realize what it was, but later that night I helped him into the garage to see it.

He sat on it and smiled — genuinely happy.

I took a picture and sent it to his friends.

Bobby was on hospice for three months — not the one week they had predicted. I was grateful for every single day.

Father's Day came, and I invited the entire family over. He rode his scooter outside, smiling, soaking it all in. On the Fourth of July, family came again. He was excited about the food. I saved him some. By then, he was eating less. He rode the scooter briefly — maybe ten minutes — before needing to lie back down.

Little by little, he slowed.
Eating less.
Talking less.

I did everything I could, alongside the nurses.

My birthday was July 12 — a Friday. Birthdays had always been special to Bobby. Every year, without fail, he made sure my birthday was celebrated — whether it was a surprise party or a big dinner with family and friends. He never let it pass quietly.

That year was no different.

My daughter decided to invite my girlfriends and some family over to spend the evening with me. I asked Bobby if he was okay with it. He said yes — but his eyes had that faraway look I'd come to recognize.

On July 10, I made him one of his favorite meals. He ate a little and thanked me so sincerely. While I cleaned up, my sister came over and we sat outside talking. Bobby was inside sleeping. After she left, I went to check on him. He was still asleep — but his vitals were not good.

I did everything the nurses had taught me. Nothing helped. I tried to wake him. He wouldn't wake up.

My daughter and her fiancé said, "Mom, call hospice."
I said, "What for? I'm doing everything they would do. They'll be here in the morning."

I slept in the room with him that night. He never woke up.

The nurses came the next morning — my birthday — and told me he was transitioning again. They said he might last through the weekend. They bathed him, kept him comfortable, and I played his CD — all the songs he loved hearing himself sing.

That afternoon, I sat beside him holding his hand. I told him that Brielle and I were going to be okay. That it was okay for him to let go. I asked him if he could hear me, to squeeze my hand. He did.

I called the priest. They came and read his last rites with our family surrounding him. And shortly after that, Bobby passed away.

On my birthday.

Bobby didn't just leave me with memories.

He left me with a birthday that would forever remind me how deeply I was loved—and how even in loss, God still gave me a gift.

Friends and family took care of everything that needed to be done. Everyone said their goodbyes. I sat with him in disbelief, crying, until the funeral home came.

I'll never forget going into the bathroom to wash my face. Standing there, head down, crying in front of the mirror — and feeling him behind me. His arms wrapped around me.

It was so real.

I know it was him.

For months, I prayed every single day for a miracle. I begged God to heal him, to spare him, to change the ending. And in time, I realized the miracle had already been given. The miracle wasn't that Bobby was healed — it was that he came home. That we had time. That he wasn't alone in a hospital room, but surrounded by love, laughter, music, family, and friends. God answered my prayers — just not in the way I expected. And that miracle will forever be one of the greatest gifts of my life.

From My Heart to Yours…

I want to speak to you gently here, because this chapter… this is sacred ground.

This is where love and loss meet in a way that words can barely hold.

If you have ever walked someone home in their final days…
If you have ever sat beside a bed, watching, waiting, praying…
If you have ever whispered words you never thought you'd have to say…

Then you understand.

There is a tenderness in this kind of love that changes you forever.

Psalm 23 says, *"He leads me beside still waters, He restores my soul."*

And I used to think that meant peace would feel calm... quiet... steady.

But sometimes, those "still waters" don't come in the way we expect.

Sometimes they come in the middle of goodbye.

Sometimes they come in the form of time...
unexpected, unearned, deeply sacred time.

Because what you may not realize while you're living it is this:

Those days—the meals, the laughter, the visitors, the moments that almost feel normal again—
they are not ordinary.

They are gifts.

They are the kind of moments that heaven touches for just a little while longer.

And if you've experienced that... if you've had even a glimpse of that kind of time...

Then you have witnessed something holy.

There is something powerful about bringing someone home.

Not just physically... but emotionally, spiritually, completely.

Home where they are surrounded by the people they love.
Home where laughter still finds its way into the room.
Home where stories are told, songs are played, and hands are held.

Home where love becomes the loudest thing in the space.

And I want to say this to you, especially if you've ever questioned whether you did enough, whether you handled it the "right" way, whether you were strong enough...

You were exactly what they needed.

Every meal you made.
Every moment you sat beside them.
Every time you learned something new, even when you felt overwhelmed.
Every tear, every prayer, every ounce of love you gave...

It mattered.

More than you will ever fully understand.

Because in the end, what people remember... what they feel... is love.

Not perfection.
Not whether everything went according to plan.

Love.

And you gave that—fully, completely, sacrificially.

That is no small thing.

But I also want to gently speak to the part of your heart that may still carry a quiet question...

Why didn't the miracle come the way I asked for it?

Because if you're honest, you prayed.

You believed.
You asked God to heal, to intervene, to change the outcome.

And when the ending looks different than what you hoped for, it can leave a space in your heart that feels hard to explain.

But what if...

What if the miracle wasn't in the outcome...
but in the time?

The extra days.
The shared meals.
The laughter that still found its way into the room.
The moments where you got to say what needed to be said.

The chance to walk with them... all the way to the edge... without them being alone.

That is a kind of grace that not everyone receives.

And I believe with all my heart—that was God.

Not absent.
Not ignoring your prayers.

But answering them in a way that held both love and mercy.

Because sometimes healing doesn't look like staying.

Sometimes healing looks like peace.

And sometimes love… the deepest, most selfless kind of love… looks like letting go.

Even when every part of you wants to hold on.

And I know how hard that is.

But I also know this…

Love does not end in that moment.

It doesn't disappear when the room goes quiet.
It doesn't fade when their voice is no longer heard the same way.

It changes.

It becomes something you carry.

In your memories.
In your heart.
In the way you live your life moving forward.

And sometimes—if you're open to it—you will feel it.

In a moment you can't quite explain.
In a sense of presence that wraps around you when you need it most.
In a memory that feels so real it brings both tears and comfort at the same time.

That is not something to question.

That is something to receive.

Because love that deep… doesn't just disappear.

It lingers.
It surrounds.
It stays.

And you—whether you feel ready or not—are still here.

Still breathing.
Still living.
Still carrying a story that is not over.

This is where reinvention begins in one of the most tender ways.

Not with big steps.
Not with bold declarations.

But with a quiet realization…

I am still here.

And because you are still here…

There is still purpose in your life.
There is still love for you to give and receive.
There are still moments ahead that will hold meaning, even if they look different than before.

You are not leaving your past behind.

You are carrying it forward in a new way.

With deeper compassion.
With greater understanding.
With a heart that knows both love and loss—and still chooses to keep going.

So if you are in this space... this tender, sacred, in-between place...

Let me say this to you softly:

You did not lose everything.

You were given something that will stay with you forever.

And God... in His quiet, gentle way...

Is still leading you.

Still restoring you.

Still guiding you beside still waters—

Even here.

Chapter 7

Still Standing

"The Lord is close to the brokenhearted and saves those who are crushed in spirit." -Psalm 34:18

AS THE WEEKS went by and much of the noise faded, the quiet settled in—and that's when things felt the hardest.

Day-to-day tasks felt almost impossible. Simple things required effort I didn't feel I had. It was surreal to be living in a world where I was still here, still breathing, still showing up—while Bobby was not. I kept thinking, How is this real?

There were responsibilities I had to take care of—things I had never done before, things Bobby had always handled. I didn't always know how, but I showed up anyway. Some days, just showing up felt like a victory.

Around that same time, my friend Laurie—who had become sick with cancer while Bobby was still in the hospital—began taking a turn for the worse. I would go visit her, sit with her, talk with her, and a few times even help with her care. It felt familiar in a way I wasn't ready for. Too familiar. Grief seemed to be following me, one door after another.

Not long after, my cousin invited my daughter and me to Puerto Rico for a week, offering us their condo. I was grateful beyond words. We went, and we truly did have a wonderful time. It was beautiful—sun, ocean, laughter, moments where my heart felt a little lighter.

And yet, through all of it, the same thought kept returning.

Bobby should be here.

Still, I was deeply grateful to my cousins for opening their home to us and giving us that time away. It mattered more than they'll ever know.

Around that same period, I decided to start some renovations on my house—things Bobby and I had talked about doing together. It felt like a way to keep moving forward while still honoring what we had planned. When we returned from Puerto Rico, I dove into that project.

At the same time, my mother-in-law began calling me more often to check on how I was doing. Her own health was declining, and I was trying to help her figure out nursing care at home. We talked constantly. She worried about me more than herself.

Then, shortly after returning from Puerto Rico, she called and told me she needed me there.

I booked a trip for four days later.

Before I could leave, Laurie took another turn for the worse. I stayed at her house, keeping her company, giving her daughters a break when they needed it. It was heartbreaking. I promised them that when I returned from helping my mother-in-law, I would come back and help again.

When I arrived in California, it was clear my mother-in-law wasn't doing well. She was on oxygen and struggled to move around. Still, we shared dinner together. She even asked for a beer with her meal. We talked for hours—about life, about memories, about everything and nothing. She was so concerned about me.

I had two days with her where she was fully coherent.

On the third day, I helped her out of bed and into the chair she loved to sit in. She slept most of the day. That night, my sister-in-law arrived. Somehow, my mother-in-law sensed her presence. She reached for both of our hands and told us she loved us.

The next morning, she was still sleeping.

We called hospice. They said they would arrive in a couple of hours. I knew—deep down—that it was a matter of hours or days.

I stepped outside and said a prayer. I asked God if my husband or my father-in-law was there—to please take her peacefully.

As I prayed, a white feather floated down and landed at my feet.

My sister-in-law and I took turns showering. When I came out, she told me hospice had arrived. I went into the room, spoke to my mother-in-law, and held her hand.

She passed while I was holding it.

There were arrangements to make, affairs to settle. We stayed almost a full week to take care of everything.

Two days before I was scheduled to return home, my phone rang.

It was Laurie's daughters.

They called to tell me that Laurie had passed away.

When they say things come in threes, they sure do.

I had barely wrapped my heart around losing my husband when grief came back again—then again—without warning. It felt relentless, like waves that didn't give me enough time to catch my breath before the next one hit.

Bobby.
Laurie.
My mother-in-law.

Three losses in such a short span of time.

There were moments I honestly wondered how much a heart could take and still keep beating. I wasn't just grieving—I was absorbing grief for everyone around me, holding space for others while my own was cracked wide open.

And yet, somehow, I was still standing.

Not because I felt strong.
Not because I had it all together.

But because love had trained my heart to keep showing up, even when it hurt.

I didn't understand why God allowed so much loss all at once. I didn't have answers—only questions and tears and a faith that felt bruised but not broken. What I did know was this: even in the middle of unimaginable pain, I wasn't abandoned.

Every time I thought I couldn't handle one more thing, I was carried through it—sometimes by people, sometimes by prayer, sometimes by signs that reminded me I wasn't alone.

Grief changed me.

But it didn't end me.

Grief does not follow a schedule, and healing does not happen in a straight line. In seasons where loss seems to stack one heartbreak on top of another, God does not step back—He steps closer.

I learned that strength isn't loud or polished. Sometimes strength looks like showing up when you don't have answers. It looks like loving others while your own heart is breaking. It looks like trusting God even when you don't understand why so much is being asked of you all at once.

This chapter of my life taught me that being "crushed in spirit" does not mean being abandoned. It means being held—sometimes quietly, sometimes painfully, but never alone.

And even when grief comes in threes, God's presence remains constant.

From My Heart to Yours…

I want to sit with you here, because this chapter… this is what it looks like to keep going when your heart doesn't feel ready.

This is what it looks like to still be standing.

Not strong in the way the world defines strength…
But standing in a way only someone who has walked through deep loss can understand.

If you have ever found yourself in a season where the world keeps moving, but your heart is still trying to catch up…

You know this feeling.

The quiet after everything.
The space where the visitors go home, the phone stops ringing as much, and life expects you to somehow return to "normal."

But nothing feels normal.

The simplest things feel heavy.
The smallest decisions feel overwhelming.
And there's this quiet, constant thought:

How is this my life now?

Psalm 34:18 says, *"The Lord is close to the brokenhearted and saves those who are crushed in spirit."*

Crushed.

Not just hurting.
Not just sad.

Crushed.

That word gives permission to the depth of what you may be feeling.

Because sometimes grief doesn't come gently.

Sometimes it comes in waves...
And then another wave...
And then another... before you've even had time to breathe.

Loss stacked on loss.
Heartbreak layered on heartbreak.

And you find yourself wondering...

How much can one heart hold?

If you've asked that question, I want you to know—you are not alone in it.

And there is nothing weak about you for feeling that way.

In fact, the very fact that you are still here... still showing up... still loving others even in the middle of your own pain...

That is a strength most people will never fully understand.

But I want to gently shift something for you.

Because when we walk through seasons like this, it's easy to start believing that strength looks like holding it all together.

That if you're falling apart, questioning, crying, or just barely getting through the day... something must be wrong.

But what if strength actually looks like this:

Getting out of bed when you didn't want to.
Making the call you didn't know how to make.
Showing up for someone else when your own heart is tired.
Taking the next step... even when you don't feel ready.

That is strength.

Quiet.
Unseen.
But incredibly powerful.

And here's something else I want you to hold onto...

Grief changing you does not mean it is breaking you beyond repair.

It is shaping you.

Deepening you.

Expanding your capacity to feel, to love, to understand life in a way you couldn't before.

And I know—that doesn't always feel like a gift.

Sometimes it just feels heavy.

But even here... God is present.

Not waiting for you to "get through it."
Not expecting you to have answers.

But walking with you in it.

Isaiah 41:10 says, *"Do not fear, for I am with you... I will strengthen you and help you; I will uphold you with my righteous right hand."*

Uphold.

That means when you feel like you can't stand on your own...

You are being held up.

And sometimes, that doesn't just come from God in a way we can see or feel directly.

It comes through people.
Through moments.
Through small, unexpected signs that remind you...

You are not alone.

Even when it feels like it.

And maybe you've had moments like that.

A conversation that came at just the right time.
A person who showed up without you asking.
A sign—something simple, something unexplainable—that made you pause and feel... seen.

Those moments matter.

They are reminders.

That even in the middle of overwhelming loss...

You are still being cared for.

You are still being guided.

You are still being held.

And I know there may still be questions sitting in your heart...

Why so much at once?
Why didn't I have more time?
Why does it feel like I didn't even get a chance to catch my breath?

Those questions are real.

And it's okay if you don't have answers.

Faith does not require you to understand everything.

Sometimes faith simply says...

God, I don't understand this... but I trust that You are still here.

And that kind of faith—even when it feels fragile—is incredibly powerful.

Because here you are.

Still standing.

Not untouched.
Not unchanged.

But still here.

Still breathing.
Still moving forward, one step at a time.

And that means something.

It means your story is not over.

It means there is still purpose in your life.
Still love to give.
Still moments ahead that will carry meaning—even if they look different than before.

Reinvention, in this season, doesn't look like big moves or bold decisions.

It looks like quiet resilience.

It looks like choosing to keep going... even when it's hard.
It looks like allowing yourself to feel... and still taking the next step.

It looks like becoming someone who has walked through deep loss...

And still believes there is life ahead.

So if you are in a season where grief feels heavy, where life feels unfamiliar, where you're not sure how you're still standing...

Let me say this to you, clearly and gently:

You are not standing alone.

God is closer than you think.
Stronger than you feel.
And still writing something meaningful with your life.

Even here.

Especially here.

Because reinvention is not the absence of pain.

It is the quiet, powerful truth that...

Even after everything...

You are still standing.

Chapter 8

Carrying Love Forward

"The Lord gives strength to His people; the Lord blesses His people with peace." - Psalm 29:11

MY FIRST HOLIDAYS without my husband were hard.

But if I'm being honest, I think I was still numb.

They came and went like a blur.

Sam came over and helped me put up the Christmas tree. I remember standing there while we untangled lights and pulled ornaments out of boxes that held decades of memories. Some ornaments made me smile. Others made my chest tighten. The house looked festive, but it didn't feel the same. There was an emptiness in the room that no amount of lights could fill.

Still, I was grateful. Grateful I wasn't alone. Grateful someone cared enough to step into the quiet with me.

I hosted my annual Christmas Eve dinner with my family. I cooked. I set the table. I welcomed everyone in. I smiled in the pictures.

But inside, I felt like I was watching myself from the outside — playing the role I had always played, just without him beside me.

After the holidays, when the decorations came down and the house grew still again, reality felt heavier. I stayed busy finishing projects around the house, organizing, planning, trying to think about what was next.

That was the hardest part — moving forward.

Every time I did something new or made a decision, it hit me like a ton of bricks:

I'm doing this without my husband.

Even the smallest moments carried weight.

One night, some friends asked me to go out to dinner. I stood in my room getting dressed, staring at my reflection, unsure of what I was even feeling. I didn't know if I should go. I didn't know if I was ready.

As I was getting ready, my cousin called. The moment I heard her voice, I broke down crying.

I told her how strange it all felt. How weird it was to even think about going out and laughing. I didn't want to feel happy. I didn't know if I was allowed to. It almost felt like betrayal.

That was the part no one talks about — the guilt of feeling even a flicker of joy.

When you've loved deeply, happiness after loss can feel disloyal. As if smiling means you're forgetting. As if laughing means you're moving on too fast. As if peace somehow replaces love.

It doesn't.

But grief can whisper lies that make you question everything.

I told my cousin I didn't want to look happy. I didn't want people to think I was "okay." Because I wasn't okay. I was still grieving. Still hurting. Still missing him in every room.

And then she said something that stopped me.

"Celinda… you're looking for peace."

She was right.

Not happiness.
Not distraction.
Not pretending everything was fine.

Peace.

The kind of peace that lets you breathe without guilt.
The kind of peace that doesn't erase love but steadies your heart.
The kind of peace that reminds you it's okay to live again.

I realized I wasn't trying to replace anything. I wasn't trying to outrun grief. I just didn't want to feel torn inside every time I stepped into the world.

And that night, I went to dinner.

Not because I felt joyful.
Not because I felt healed.
But because I was beginning to understand something important:

Moving forward didn't mean leaving him behind.

It meant learning how to carry him with me — without letting guilt steal the life I was still meant to live.

One of the hardest parts of grief is allowing yourself to feel moments of peace again. After losing someone you love deeply, even small moments of happiness can feel like betrayal. But healing does not mean forgetting. Love does not disappear when someone is gone—it changes the way it lives within us. I learned that moving forward wasn't about leaving Bobby behind or pretending everything was okay. It was about learning to carry the love we shared into the next chapter of my life. Peace is not disloyal to love; in many ways, it is love continuing to guide us forward.

From My Heart to Yours…

I want to sit with you here, because this chapter holds a kind of quiet ache that so many women carry… but don't always have words for.

This is the space where life begins again—but your heart isn't quite sure how to follow.

The holidays, the gatherings, the moments that used to feel full…
they come around again, but everything feels different.

You show up.
You go through the motions.
You smile when you're supposed to smile.

But inside… it's not the same.

And if you've ever felt like you were watching your own life from the outside—like you're there, but not fully there—you are not alone in that.

Grief has a way of doing that.

It doesn't just take someone you love.
It changes how you experience everything.

Psalm 29:11 says, *"The Lord gives strength to His people; the Lord blesses His people with peace."*

And I think sometimes we misunderstand what that peace looks like.

We think it will feel like everything is okay again.
Like the ache will disappear.
Like the heaviness will lift all at once.

But often... peace comes much more gently than that.

It comes in moments.

A breath where your chest doesn't feel so tight.
A conversation where you forget, just for a second, how heavy everything is.
A small step forward that doesn't feel quite as impossible as it did the day before.

And sometimes... it comes with tears.

Because one of the hardest parts of this season—the part not many people talk about—is the guilt.

The guilt of laughing.
The guilt of going out.
The guilt of feeling even a small spark of something that resembles joy.

It can feel like betrayal.

Like if you allow yourself to feel okay… even for a moment… you are somehow leaving them behind.

But I want to gently tell you something that may set your heart free:

Peace is not betrayal.

It is permission.

Permission to breathe again.
Permission to step into life again.
Permission to carry love forward instead of feeling like you have to leave it behind.

Because you are not replacing what you had.

You are honoring it.

Every time you show up.
Every time you take a step forward.
Every time you allow yourself—even cautiously—to live again.

That is not forgetting.

That is remembering in a new way.

John 14:27 says, *"Peace I leave with you; my peace I give you... Do not let your hearts be troubled and do not be afraid."*

Not the world's version of peace.
Not a forced happiness or a pretending everything is fine.

But a deeper peace.

The kind that sits quietly in your spirit and says:

You can take the next step.
You can go to dinner.
You can laugh again... and it doesn't mean you loved any less.

Because the truth is...

Love that deep does not disappear when someone is gone.

It changes form.

It becomes something you carry into every room.
Every conversation.
Every decision.

You don't walk forward alone.

You walk forward with everything they gave you.

And yes... it will feel strange at first.

The first time you go out.
The first time you laugh.
The first time you realize you made it through a moment without thinking of them every second.

Those moments can feel confusing.

But they are also signs of something important:

You are still alive.

And your life... still has meaning.

Reinvention in this season doesn't look loud or bold.

It looks like this:

Standing in your room, unsure—but getting ready anyway.
Walking into a space that feels unfamiliar—and staying.
Allowing yourself to feel something other than grief—and not running from it.

It looks like choosing peace... even when it feels unfamiliar.

And if you are standing in that space right now—torn between honoring what was and stepping into what is—let me say this to you clearly:

You are allowed to live again.

You are allowed to feel peace.
You are allowed to laugh.
You are allowed to experience moments of light... even after deep loss.

That does not diminish your love.

It reflects it.

Because the love you shared was never meant to keep you stuck.

It was meant to strengthen you… carry you… and become part of the life you continue to live.

So if tonight, or tomorrow, or sometime soon, you find yourself standing in front of a mirror wondering if you're ready…

You don't have to be fully ready.

You just have to be willing.

Willing to take one step.
Willing to breathe a little deeper.
Willing to let peace find you… even in small ways.

Because God is not asking you to forget your past.

He is gently leading you forward—
with love still in your heart,
and peace slowly, faithfully… finding its way in.

Chapter 9

A God Wink

"The Lord makes firm the steps of the one who delights in Him."
— Psalm 37:23

SOMETIMES WHEN I LOOK BACK over my life, I realize that the moments that seemed random at the time were anything but random.

They were God moments.

The kind people sometimes call a *God wink*—those small, unexpected events that later reveal themselves as part of a much bigger plan.

Before Bobby and I ever dated, before we built a life together, before all the memories that would shape my heart forever... there was a moment that neither of us could have imagined would connect our lives.

I knew *of* Bobby before I really knew him. He was in a band, and like many people in the area, I had heard about him. One night

I was out with my girlfriends while his band was playing. We were laughing—really laughing—the kind of carefree laughter you have when you're young and the night feels endless.

At some point Bobby stopped what he was doing and looked over.

Apparently, he turned to the people around him and said, "Who is that laughing? That's the girl I'm going to marry."

Of course, I had no idea what he said that at the time.

And if I had heard it, I probably would have rolled my eyes. In fact, the first impression I had of him back then was that he seemed a little arrogant. Life has a funny way of changing first impressions.

Not long after that night, something happened that none of us expected. One evening my parents were driving home late at night after being out themselves. As they were driving, they happened to be behind a car that had just left a nightclub where a band had been playing. They didn't realize at the time whose car it was.

As they approached a traffic light, my parents noticed a police car nearby and slowed down. The car ahead of them went through the light. Then suddenly, there was an accident.

Another car had swerved into the lane. Later they would learn the woman driving had fallen asleep behind the wheel. My parents pulled over immediately and rushed to help.

My father got out of the car and ran toward the vehicle. When he reached the driver, he placed his hand on the man's leg to check for a pulse. He could feel it. The man was alive. He was moaning, injured but breathing.

My father later told me that when he went to check the other car, he knew instantly that the woman inside had already passed away. My parents helped call the police and the ambulance. Once help was on the way, they eventually left and went home.

When they told me about the accident later, I listened but didn't think much of it. I didn't even know who had been involved. Life simply moved on. Months passed—six or eight months passed, maybe more.

One night I happened to be out again with some friends, and Bobby's band was playing. I didn't think much of it until he came up to me.

He said,
"I heard that your parents were the ones who stopped and called the police and ambulance the night of my accident. I just wanted to thank you… and thank them."

That's when it all connected. The man my parents had stopped to help that night was Bobby.

If they had taken a different road…
If they had left a few minutes earlier…
If they had slowed down or sped up at the wrong moment…

Our paths might never have crossed. But they did.

From that moment on, Bobby and I began talking more. We weren't immediately dating or anything like that. At first, we were simply friendlier with each other. Conversations became easier. We laughed. We got to know each other little by little.

And over time, those conversations turned into something more. Looking back now, it's impossible for me not to see God's hand in that moment. What were the odds?

That my parents would be the ones behind him that night.
That they would be the ones to stop.
That months later we would reconnect and realize the connection between us.

It was as if God had quietly written the beginning of our story long before either of us realized it. At the time, it just felt like coincidence. Now I know better. It was the very first page of a love story I would carry with me for the rest of my life.

Sometimes the most important relationships in our lives begin in ways we never could have planned. Moments that seem like coincidence are often part of a much bigger story that only God can see in full.

Looking back, I realize that the night of Bobby's accident wasn't just a frightening moment, it was the first thread that would weave our lives together. God often works quietly, arranging people and moments long before we understand why.

And sometimes what looks like chance…
is the beginning of a blessing we never saw coming.

From My Heart to Yours…

When I look back at how Bobby and I met, I can't help but smile… and shake my head a little. Because if I'm being honest, nothing about it felt extraordinary at the time.

It felt random.
It felt like coincidence.
It felt like just another night, just another story.

But now I know… it was anything but that. It was God. And if you're reading this right now, I want you to pause for just a moment and think about your own life. Have you ever had a moment that didn't make sense at the time…
but later, when you looked back, you could see how everything lined up perfectly?

A conversation. A delay. A person you almost didn't meet. A moment you almost missed. Those are the moments we often overlook. But those are the moments where God is quietly working.

Psalm 37:23 says, *"The Lord makes firm the steps of the one who delights in Him."*
And I didn't always understand that verse the way I do now.

Because sometimes those "steps" don't feel firm at all. Sometimes they feel uncertain. Unplanned. Even inconvenient. But what I've come to realize is this:
God is often writing something beautiful in the background... long before we see the full picture.

When my parents stopped that night to help at the accident, they weren't thinking about me. They weren't thinking about a future. They were simply doing what was right in the moment.

But God was already connecting the dots. He was already writing a story. A story that would lead me to the man I would love, build a life with, and carry in my heart forever. And here's what I want you to hear—especially if you are in a season of reinvention, loss, or uncertainty:

God is still writing your story too.

Even in the moments that feel random.
Even in the moments that feel painful.
Even in the moments that feel like nothing is happening at all.

Especially in those moments. Sometimes we think our story starts when everything finally makes sense. But the truth is... the most important parts of our story are often being written when we don't understand it yet. When you're walking through something hard, it's easy to ask:

Why is this happening?
Where is this going?
What does this even mean?

I've asked those questions too. But looking back now, I see something I didn't see then: God was present in the beginning... and He was present all the way through. That "God wink" moment the night everything connected—it wasn't just about how Bobby and I met. It was a reminder that our lives are not random. That love is not random. That the people we are meant to meet, the paths we are meant to walk, and even the timing of it all... is held in God's hands.

And maybe right now, you're in a chapter where things don't make sense.

Maybe you're wondering how you got here.
Maybe you're questioning what comes next.
Maybe you're trying to piece together a story that feels broken or unfinished.

If that's you, I want to gently remind you:

Just because you can't see the plan... doesn't mean there isn't one.

There was a time when I didn't know Bobby.
There was a time when that accident was just a story my parents told.
There was a time when none of it seemed connected.

But it was. And your story is too. God doesn't waste moments. He doesn't waste connections.
He doesn't waste the things that feel small or insignificant. He weaves them together in ways only He can.

So if you are in a season of waiting... trust that something is being formed.
If you are in a season of loss... trust that love is still part of your story.
If you are in a season of reinvention... trust that this is not the end—this is a continuation.

Because sometimes what feels like an ending...
is actually the very beginning of something you couldn't have planned on your own. And one day, you will look back at a moment you almost missed...
and realize:

That was never random.

That was God.

And He's still writing your story.

Chapter 10

Finding My Way Forward

"Commit to the Lord whatever you do, and He will establish your plans."
— Proverbs 16:3

A FEW YEARS BEFORE Bobby got sick, something had been stirring in my heart.

It wasn't loud.
It wasn't urgent.
Just a quiet thought that kept returning.

What would I do if something ever happened to Bobby?

For most of our marriage, I had worked on and off. Bobby was self-employed, and we had built a life where I didn't always need to work full time. But as the years passed, I began thinking more seriously about the future.

We didn't have huge savings. And at one point we tried to increase Bobby's life insurance policy, but because of his health we couldn't. That reality stayed in the back of my mind.

One day I was talking with a friend who was a real estate agent. She said something simple that stuck with me.

"You would be good at this."

At first, I laughed it off. But the more I thought about it, the more it made sense. I liked people. I liked helping. And I knew that if something ever happened, I needed a way to support myself. So, in 2018, I decided to do it. I went to school. I studied. I took the test. And just like that, I became a licensed real estate agent.

At first it was just me learning the ropes, trying to figure things out one step at a time. I worked at it for about a year. Then COVID hit, and like so many things in life, everything slowed down.

Just when things started opening back up and I thought, *okay, it's time to really get moving again,* life threw another curveball. I broke my ankle.

Not a small break either. I ended up needing two surgeries and couldn't put weight on it for nearly six months. I was rolling around on one of those knee scooters just trying to get through the day.

During that time, something unexpected happened. A cousin of mine had gotten his real estate license too. As we talked more, we realized that maybe we could work together. And that's exactly what we did.

In 2021 we joined a brokerage as a team. It was a perfect partnership. I was the one out front connecting with people, bringing in clients, showing homes. My cousin John was incredible with negotiations and paperwork.

Everything we did, we split right down the middle. It didn't matter who brought in the client or who did which task—we were a team. And for a while, things were going well.

Then Bobby got sick. The moment we heard the words *Stage Four Cancer*, everything else in my life stopped. Real estate didn't matter. Work didn't matter. Nothing mattered except him. From January of 2024 forward, I didn't work at all. For three months I lived at the hospital.

Then Bobby came home on hospice, and for another three months my entire world became caring for him, sitting beside him, making meals, holding his hand, cherishing every moment we had left.

After he passed, I had nothing left in me to give.

Work felt impossible.
Motivation felt impossible.
Even getting out of bed some days felt like more than I could manage.

Then the holidays came and went. One day my dad sat down and talked with me. My father has always been someone I look to when it comes to business and practical things. But more than that, he was Bobby's best friend. Their bond was something special.

My family has always looked out for me. My dad gently said, "Celinda... you need to start thinking about getting back to work."

I knew he was right. But knowing something and feeling ready for it are two very different things.

"I know, Dad," I told him. "I'm just not there yet."

And for a while, I wasn't. Then March came. For years, Bobby and I traveled to Florida every March to visit close friends. That trip had become a tradition for us. This time, I went alone.

It was bittersweet in every sense of the word. There were moments of laughter and sunshine... and there were nights when I cried harder than I had in a long time. My friends were incredible. They didn't try to stop my tears or rush me through them.

They simply sat with me. Sometimes that's the greatest gift someone can give you. When I returned home at the end of March, something inside me shifted. Not completely healed.
Not suddenly strong. But ready for the next step.

I made an appointment with my broker and said,
"I think I'm ready to start working again."

Around that same time, my cousin John had decided to move in a different direction professionally. He joined another brokerage and began focusing more on construction work. There were no hard feelings at all. Life just led him down a different path. But suddenly, I was on my own.

And to be honest... I was terrified.

John had always handled the paperwork. He was so fast and so confident with it. Now I had to do everything myself—meeting clients, negotiating deals, managing contracts, hosting open houses. I remember thinking,

Can I really do this by myself?

But once again, God started placing people in my path. My cousin in Long Island—who is also a realtor—became an incredible support. When I told her how nervous I was about managing everything, especially the paperwork, she listened patiently.

A few days later, a package arrived at my house. Inside was an Apple air iPad she had sent me so I could run my business more easily. That meant more to me than she will probably ever know.

She also introduced me to a faith group called Live Out Loud, which helped strengthen my spiritual life during a season when I needed it most. My girlfriends stepped in too, helping me learn different parts of the business and cheering me on.

Slowly, I started putting the pieces together. One day I got a Zillow call from a potential buyer. I set the appointment, showed them the house, and they decided they wanted to buy it.

Right there in the middle of the showing, I started crying. I was so embarrassed. I apologized and explained my story—how my husband had passed away not long before and that I was just getting back into work.

The woman looked at me with such kindness. She was a sweet Greek woman and she said,

“Don’t worry. You’re beautiful. You’ll find someone else.”

I had to laugh through my tears That wasn’t why I was crying. But her kindness meant the world to me. And that moment turned out to be the beginning of something bigger than I expected.

That was April. By May, I had my first listing. By the end of May, I had four sales under contract. And from April through December, I closed thirteen transactions. Looking back now, I can see something I couldn’t fully see at the time.

God wasn't just helping me survive my grief. He was helping me rebuild my life.

One step.
One client.
One showing at a time.

Sometimes rebuilding life after loss feels overwhelming. The path forward can look uncertain, unfamiliar, and even frightening.

But God often provides what we need exactly when we need it—through people who support us, opportunities that appear unexpectedly, and small moments of courage that lead to bigger ones.

I learned that moving forward doesn't mean forgetting the past. It means honoring the love you shared while trusting that God still has purpose for the life you are living.

And sometimes the very thing you feared you couldn't do…

Becomes the way God reminds you that you are stronger than you ever imagined.

From My Heart to Yours…

There is something about starting over that feels both terrifying and sacred at the same time.

If you've ever found yourself standing in the middle of a life you didn't expect—where the future to look different than you imagined, you understand this feeling. Starting again is rarely dramatic. Most of the time, it happens quietly.

It happens the first time you wake up and realize you have to make decisions on your own.
It happens the first time you try something new without the person who used to stand beside you.
It happens the moment you take one small step forward, even though your heart still feels heavy.

That's what rebuilding looks like. Not giant leaps. Just small, brave steps. Sometimes we think faith means having a clear plan or feeling confident about the road ahead. But often faith looks very different. Sometimes faith is simply saying,

"God, I don't know how I'm going to do this... but I'm willing to try."

And then take the next step anyway. Proverbs reminds us, *"Commit to the Lord whatever you do, and He will establish your plans."* Notice it doesn't say we must have everything figured out before we begin. It simply says commit. Show up. Take the step that is in front of you. Trust that God will meet you there.

For many women, especially in the second half of life, reinvention comes unexpectedly. It might come after loss, after a major life transition, or after years spent caring for others before finally turning attention toward your own future. And when that moment comes, fear often shows up first.

Fear of making mistakes. Fear of being alone. Fear of stepping into something unfamiliar. But what I've learned—and what I hope you will remember—is this: Fear does not mean you are not ready.

Sometimes fear simply means you are stepping into something new. God rarely asks us to walk paths that feel comfortable from the beginning. Instead, He walks with us as we grow into them.

He sends people at the right moments.
A friend who offers encouragement.
A family member who believes in you.
A conversation that nudges you forward.

Those moments are not accidents. They are reminders that you are not walking alone. If you are reading this while standing in a season of rebuilding—emotionally, spiritually, or even professionally, I want you to know something important:

You do not have to be fully healed to begin again. You can carry your memories with you. You can still miss the life you once had. You can still have days where grief catches you off guard. And yet... you can still move forward.

Healing and rebuilding often happen side by side. One small step leads to another. One opportunity opens the door to the next. And before you realize it, you begin to see something you didn't expect. Strength.

Not the loud kind. Not the kind that pretends everything is fine. But the quiet strength that grows inside a woman who has walked through loss and chosen to keep going.

And that kind of strength is powerful. Because it means that your story isn't over.

There is still purpose in your life. There are still people you will help.
There are still experiences waiting for you that will surprise you in the best possible way. Sometimes the very path we were afraid to take becomes the one that leads us to who we were meant to become.

So, if you are standing at the beginning of something new, unsure of your footing, wondering if you have what it takes... Let me gently remind you: You do. Take the next step. God will meet you there.

And just like so many women before you, you may look back one day and realize that what once felt impossible... Was simply the beginning of your next chapter.

Chapter 11

Faith Over Fear

"For God has not given us a spirit of fear, but of power and of love and of a sound mind."
— 2 Timothy 1:7

AS THE MONTHS WENT ON, something began to shift inside of me.

At first, every step forward in real estate felt terrifying. I was constantly second-guessing myself. Every client meeting, every showing, every contract felt like a test I wasn't sure I would pass.

When I worked with my cousin, we had balanced each other. If I was unsure, he knew what to do. If I hesitated, he would step in. There was always someone to bounce things off of.Now it was just me.

I remember sitting with paperwork in front of me, staring at it and thinking, *What if I mess this up? What if I get something wrong?* But one day, I completed my first contract completely on my own. I had a friend nearby just in case I needed guidance, but I did the work myself. When it was finished, I remember staring at the documents and thinking,

Oh my goodness... I did it.

It may sound small to someone else, but to me it was huge. That moment was the beginning of something new. Little by little, the fear started to fade. The more I worked, the more confident I became. The calls came in. The showings happened. The contracts started stacking up. And at some point, I found myself wondering about something that surprised me.

Where is this confidence coming from?

Because the truth was, it didn't feel like it was coming from me alone. During that time, I had started praying more than ever before. Prayer had always been part of my life, but after everything I had been through, it became something deeper—something I leaned on every day.

Before meeting clients, I would pray. Before answering calls, I would pray. Sometimes I would say the Prayer of Jabez, asking God to bless the work of my hands and expand the opportunities in front of me. And more than once, something remarkable happened. I would finish praying... and then the phone would ring. Someone looking to buy a house. Someone needing help selling. A new opportunity appears at just the right moment.

Each time it happened, I felt the same quiet reminder in my heart:

God was still guiding my steps.

Around that same time, something else caught my attention. One day I saw a video about writing a book through CFI Publishing. At first, I wasn't sure what to think. Writing a book has never really been part of my plan. But the idea stayed with me. The more I thought about it, the more I realized something important about the journey I had been on.

For months, I had been living with fear.

Fear of the future.
Fear of being alone.
Fear of making mistakes.
Fear of whether I could rebuild my life without Bobby beside me.

But somehow, along the way, something had changed. That fear had slowly begun turning into faith.

Faith that I could figure things out.
Faith that I was stronger than I realized.
Faith that God was still opening doors in front of me.

Faith over fear.

That realization is what made me decide to write. Because if my story could help even one person move from fear to faith, then every difficult step along the way would have meaning. Around that time, I was also participating in a program called *Live Out Loud*, where we spent time reflecting on an important question:

What is your why? That question stayed with me. For most of my life, my family had always taken care of me. When Bobby was sick, they were there every day. When I felt like I was drowning in grief, they held me up. My parents, especially my dad, were always my steady ground.

My dad has always been my hero. He was not only my father, but Bobby's best friend too. They shared a bond that meant everything to both of them.

As my parents have gotten older, something inside of me shifted. For the first time in my life, I wanted to be the one taking care of them. That became my "why."

I wanted to work hard so that I could give back to the people who had carried me through some of the hardest moments of my life. One of the things I was able to do was take them on a trip to Puerto Rico—something they had always dreamed about but had never done.

When I surprised them with it, they were overwhelmed.

"Oh wow, Celinda," they said.

But to me, it wasn't a big gesture. It was simply love returning full circle. It was my why! It was my way of saying thank you. Looking back now, I realize something powerful.

The same God who carried me through grief...
was now guiding me into purpose.

The same faith that helped me survive loss...
was now helping me build a future.

And the fear that once felt so overwhelming...

had quietly turned into confidence I never knew I had.

Fear often shows up when we step into something new, especially after loss. It whispers that we aren't ready, that we might fail, or that we can't do it alone.

But faith changes the conversation.

When we trust God with the next step—even when we feel uncertain—He often provides the strength, opportunities, and people we need along the way.

I learned that courage doesn't mean the absence of fear. It means choosing faith anyway.

And sometimes the very journey that scares us the most…

becomes the one that reveals who we were meant to become.

From My Heart to Yours…

Fear has a quiet way of showing up in our lives. Sometimes it whispers. Sometimes it shouts.

It shows up when life changes suddenly. It shows up when we are asked to step into something new. And it shows up most often when we feel like we are standing alone. If you have ever found yourself staring at a decision, a new opportunity, or even a new day thinking, *what if I can't do this?*—you are not alone.

Fear often arrives right before growth. It tells us we are not ready. It tells us we might fail. It tells us we should stay where it feels safe. But God's Word reminds us of something powerful:

"For God has not given us a spirit of fear, but of power and of love and of a sound mind." (2 Timothy 1:7)

That verse doesn't mean fear will never appear in our lives. It means fear was never meant to lead us. When we walk through seasons of loss, change, or uncertainty, fear can feel overwhelming. It can make even small steps feel impossible.

But faith doesn't require us to feel fearless. Faith simply asks us to trust God enough to take the next step anyway. Sometimes that step looks small. Answering the phone.
Trying again. Saying yes to something that makes your heart nervous.

But every step forward builds confidence we didn't know we had. And often, when we look back later, we realize something beautiful: God was strengthening us all along.

Many women reach a point in life where they have to rediscover themselves. Maybe it comes after raising children, after losing someone they loved deeply, or after a major life change that forces them to begin again. That moment can feel incredibly lonely. But it is also the moment where something powerful can begin.

Because when we stop relying only on our own strength, we start leaning on something greater. Prayer becomes more than a habit. Faith becomes more than a word. It becomes a lifeline.

It becomes the quiet conversation with God before a meeting, before a decision, before stepping into something unknown. And sometimes, when we least expect it, we begin to see little reminders that we are not walking this path alone. A door opens. A phone call comes.
A person appears with encouragement at exactly the right moment.

Those moments are not accidents. They are often God reminding us that He is still guiding our steps. Faith over fear does not mean life suddenly becomes easy. It means we stop letting fear decide what we are capable of.

It means we trust that God can use even the most difficult seasons of our lives to shape something meaningful. Sometimes the very experiences that once broke our hearts become the foundation of our purpose. Sometimes the pain that once made us question everything becomes the reason, we are able to help someone else. And when that happens, we begin to see our story differently.

Not just as something we survived... but as something God is still using. If you are standing in a season where fear feels louder than faith, let me encourage you with this: You do not have to have everything figured out. You do not have to feel completely confident. You only need the courage to take the next step.

Faith grows in motion. The more we trust God with what is in front of us, the more we begin to see His hand guiding us through it. And before you know it, the fear that once felt overwhelming begins to lose its power. Not because life changed overnight. But because you did.

Because somewhere along the way, you discovered something inside yourself that you didn't realize was there. Strength. Faith. And the quiet confidence that God is still leading you forward. Even when the path is new.

Chapter 12

Still Blessed

"The Lord gives strength to His people; the Lord blesses His people with peace."
— Psalm 29:11

TODAY WHEN I LOOK AT MY LIFE, I see something I never expected to see again.

Flow.

Not the kind of life I had before.
Not the same routines or the same story.

But a new kind of rhythm.

In my work, listings started coming in one after another. Clients would call. Opportunities would appear. Some days it felt almost surreal—like the business was simply flowing to me rather than me chasing it.

And every morning when I wake up, before anything else, I stop for a moment.

I thank God.

I look around my home, my life, the people who surround me, and I think to myself:

I am so blessed.

That doesn't mean my grief is gone.

It's not.

Grief doesn't disappear when someone we love passes away. If anything, grief is proof of how deeply we loved. And I've come to understand something important about grief.

Grief is love.

It's love that no longer has a place to land in the way it once did. So it lives inside our hearts instead.

For me, Bobby's love will always live there.

I still miss him.

There are days when memories come rushing back. There are songs that still make me stop in my tracks. There are moments when I wish I could turn to him and tell him about something funny or exciting that happened.

That part never fully leaves you. But I've learned something else along the way. You don't have to live *inside* your grief. You can carry it without letting it carry you. I give myself grace when the tears come. I don't push them away. I don't pretend they don't exist.

But I also don't let grief steal the life that God has placed in front of me. Every month, on the exact date and time that Bobby passed away, I pause. No matter what I'm doing, I stop.

Sometimes I'm alone. Sometimes I'm with family or friends. We raise a glass. We say quiet cheers. Not in sadness, but in remembrance. Because Bobby loved life. He loved laughter. He loved bringing people together. And honoring him that way feels right. It reminds me that love didn't end. It simply changed form.

If there is one thing I hope you take away from my story, it's this: Life can change in an instant. One moment you are living your everyday life, making plans, laughing with the people you love... and the next moment everything looks different.

But even when life changes, God does not leave you. He walks beside you through the hospital rooms, the heartbreak, the long nights, and the quiet mornings where you wonder how you're going to get through the day.

And slowly—sometimes so slowly you barely notice—He helps you stand again.

Then one day you realize something.

You are still here.

Still loving.
Still living.

Still capable of building something meaningful with the life you have.

Reinvention doesn't erase the past.

It honors it.

Everything Bobby and I shared—the laughter, the traditions, the years of love—became the foundation that carried me forward when I thought I might fall apart.

And now, when I wake up each morning and thank God for another day, I know something with certainty:

Love never truly leaves us. It lives on in the way we keep going. In the way we care for others. In the way we choose faith over fear. So if you are reading this and walking through a season of loss, uncertainty, or reinvention, I want you to hear this clearly: You are stronger than you think.

Your story is not over.

And even when life feels broken...

God is still writing something beautiful with the pieces.

I am still standing.

Still grateful.

Still blessed.

And that, in itself, is a miracle.

Blessings can return to our lives even after deep loss. Grief does not disappear, but it can learn to live beside gratitude. I've come to understand that grief is simply love that continues after someone is gone. When we allow ourselves to remember, honor, and carry that love forward, we also make space for peace. God does not remove every sorrow from our lives, but He walks with us through it and gently leads us toward healing. In time, we discover that continuing to live, to love, and to be grateful is not forgetting—it is the greatest way to honor the love that shaped us.

From My Heart to Yours…

There is a moment that eventually comes after loss. Not a dramatic moment.
Not one where everything suddenly feels healed or resolved. But a quiet realization.

You wake up one morning and notice that life is moving again.
Not the same life you once had.
Not the life you would have chosen. But life, nonetheless.

And in that moment, something unexpected happens, you begin to see blessings again. For a while after loss, it can feel almost impossible to notice those things. Grief takes up so much space that it feels like nothing else can exist beside it.

But slowly, gently, the light begins to return. A conversation with a friend. A moment of laughter you didn't expect. A sense of peace that shows up quietly when you least expect it. These moments don't erase grief. They simply remind us that grief and gratitude can exist together.

Psalm 29:11 says, *"The Lord gives strength to His people; the Lord blesses His people with peace."*

Peace doesn't mean the absence of pain. It means the presence of God in the middle of it. And sometimes that peace shows up in the most ordinary ways—through the people who stand beside us, the opportunities that appear, and the quiet reminders that our lives still hold purpose.

One of the hardest lessons many of us learn after losing someone we love is that life continues. First that can feel unfair. How can the world keep moving when someone so important is gone? But over time, we begin to understand something deeper.

Continuing to live fully is not a betrayal of the love we shared. It is a reflection of it. The love we received from someone who meant so much to us becomes part of who we are. It shapes the way we see people. It deepens our compassion. It reminds us to treasure the small moments we once took for granted.

Love changes us. And that change stays with us long after someone is gone. If you are reading this while walking through your own season of grief, uncertainty, or reinvention, I want you to remember something important.

Your story is not over.

Even if life looks different than you imagined...
Even if the future feels unclear...
Even if some days still feel heavy...

God is still present in your life. He is still guiding your steps. Still opening doors. Still helping you discover strength you didn't know you had. Sometimes we don't recognize how far we've come until we look back and realize we survived something we once thought we couldn't.

And when that moment comes, you begin to see your life through a different lens. Not just through the pain you endured... But through the grace that carried you through it. So if today feels difficult, take it one step at a time.

If tomorrow feels uncertain, trust that God is already there. And if you ever wonder whether joy can exist again after loss, remember this: The same God who walked beside you through your darkest moments is also the one who leads you toward peace.

You are still here.

Still capable of loving.
Still capable of living.
Still capable of building something meaningful with the life in front of you.

And sometimes the greatest miracle of all is simply this: After everything...

You are still standing.

Still grateful.

Still blessed.

Acknowledgments

There are so many people who carried me through the hardest season of my life, and I would be remiss if I did not take a moment to thank them.

First, to my family.

To my mom, my dad, my aunts, uncles, and cousins—thank you for surrounding me with love through it all. Thank you for sitting beside me when I needed someone to lean on, for letting me cry on your shoulders, and for the late-night phone calls that helped me laugh again. You came to my home, made dinner, and simply sat with me so I wouldn't feel alone. Your love and support carried me in ways that words could never fully express.

To my girlfriends, who were always there by my side with a bottle of wine and plenty of laughter—thank you. Through some of the toughest days and nights, you answered phone calls, stayed up late talking with me, and reminded me that I didn't have to walk through grief alone. Those nights together—talking, laughing, and sometimes crying—meant more than you will ever know. I love my girlfriends dearly. They know who they are, and I am forever grateful for their friendship.

There are also a few very special friends of both Bobby and me who deserve recognition.

Rick and Kari were there during the hospital days almost every night, sitting with Bobby so he wouldn't be alone when I needed to go home. Rick still checks on me constantly, always asking if there is anything I need. Whether it's fixing something around my house or helping with something small, he is always there. Words simply cannot express how much I appreciate that kind of loyalty and care.

Lori has been there from the very beginning. During the hospital days, she came every morning. She brought Bobby food, his favorite treats, and gave me the chance to go home for a bit to rest or take care of things that needed to be done. Her kindness and consistency meant so much during those difficult days. Even after Bobby passed, Lori continued to show up in my life. She helped me pack some of his belongings and has never stopped checking in on me. Every month on the anniversary of his passing, she calls just to remind me that she loves me. That kind of friendship is rare, and I cherish it deeply.

To my dear friends Tony and Charlene, thank you for your constant support. Thank you for the phone calls, the dinners you brought over, and for simply being there whenever I needed it. You allowed me to grieve, to cry, and to process everything without ever making me feel uncomfortable. In many ways, I became their "plus one," and they welcomed me with open arms. Their friendship has meant more to me than they probably realize.

To everyone who stood by my side during this journey—thank you. Your love, your presence, and your kindness helped carry me through the fire. I will forever be grateful.

And finally, to my daughter, Brielle.

Words cannot fully express what she means to me. Even while going through her own grief, she held me up during moments when I didn't think I could go on. I am so incredibly proud of the woman she has become.

There were nights when I was alone and struggling, and she would make it a point to come sit with me. Sometimes we talked. Other nights we simply watched movies together, sharing quiet moments that meant more than she probably realized.

Her strength, compassion, and love carried me through some of my darkest days. I truly don't know how I would have made it through without her.

She has become my rock, and I love her more than words could ever express. I am endlessly grateful to walk this life beside her.

Photo Insert

A Note From The Author

The First Year

The one-year anniversary of Bobby's passing fell on my birthday.

That alone felt surreal. Birthdays are supposed to be a time of celebration, but that year carried a very different weight. It marked an entire year of learning how to live without the man I had shared my life with.

I decided to celebrate quietly with family and a few of our closest friends—people who had stood beside me and walked with me through the hardest year of my life.

My daughter helped me put everything together. We planned a small gathering—nothing fancy, just a moment to be together and acknowledge how far we had come.

At one point during the evening, I raised a glass and made a toast. I thanked everyone for standing by my side through that first year—through the tears, the questions, and the moments when I didn't know how I was going to get through the day.

Their love carried me when I didn't feel strong enough to carry myself.

Life, however, continued moving forward. I kept working and staying busy. In many ways, that helped me keep my footing. Work gave me purpose and structure when everything else in my life felt uncertain.

Bobby's birthday came on December 4.

Around that time, my sisters and I decided to take a trip together. It felt good to get away, to breathe a little differently, and to be surrounded by the people who knew me best. There is something about sisters that brings a comfort you can't quite explain.

But when the holidays came around again, something felt different.

In many ways, that second holiday season felt even harder than the first.

During the first year, I think I was still numb. Everything moved so quickly that it almost felt like I was watching it happen from the outside. But by the second year, reality had settled in. The permanence of the loss was clearer.

I remember cooking my Christmas Eve dinner that year, just like I had done so many times before.

The house was quiet.

Everyone was coming later, but in that moment it was just me in the kitchen, preparing the meal like I always had.

And I cried.

I cried almost the entire time I was cooking before everyone arrived.

Not because I didn't want them there, but because every memory of Christmas past seemed to walk through that kitchen with me.

The laughter.
The traditions.
The sound of Bobby's voice filling the house.

Grief has a way of showing up in the quiet moments.

And that evening, standing alone in my kitchen, it showed up in full force.

But when my family and friends arrived, something else filled the room.

Love. The kind of love that reminds you that even though someone is missing, you are not alone.

And somehow, through tears, memories, and a house full of people who cared, Christmas still happened—just in a different way than before.

The title and inspiration behind this book come from the song *Because You Loved Me* by Céline Dion. Every time I hear that song, it touches something deep in my heart. The message reminds me of the love that carried me through so many seasons of my life.

My husband believed in me when I didn't always believe in myself. He stood beside me, encouraged me, and loved me in a way that helped shape the woman I became.

Because he loved me, I learned what strength looks like. Because he loved me, I learned how to keep going when life felt

impossible.
Because he loved me, I experienced a love so powerful that it continues to carry me even after loss.

CONNECT WITH THE AUTHOR

CELINDA GOBELOFF
csells4you@gmail.com
(757) 705-8672

www.ingramcontent.com/pod-product-compliance
Lightning Source LLC
LaVergne TN
LVHW010624100826
845148LV00014B/3092

9798234008725